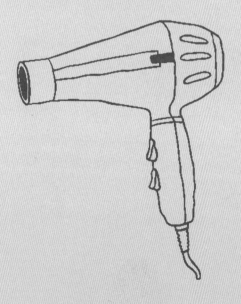

THE STORY
OF ME AND MY
MOM

First published by Parragon Books Ltd in 2013
LIFE CANVAS is an imprint of Parragon Books Ltd

Parragon
Chartist House
15-17 Trim Street
Bath BA1 1HA, UK
www.parragon.com

LIFE CANVAS and the accompanying logo are trademarks of Parragon
Books Ltd

Produced by Tall Tree Ltd
Illustrations by Apple Agency

ISBN 978-1-4723-0743-9
GTIN 5060292801032

Printed in China

This is a gift for you,
Mom, because...

love from ....

where ....

when ....

THIS IS ONE OF MY FAVORITE
PHOTOS OF THE TWO OF US

OUR JOURNEY TOGETHER

THIS THREAD RUNS THROUGH THE BOOK AND LINKS PHOTOS THAT SHOW THE THINGS WE'VE DONE TOGETHER OVER THE YEARS.

stick your photo here

MOM, I'VE GIVEN YOU A SCORE FROM 1–10
FOR EACH OF THESE

Kind	1 2 3 4 5 6 7 8 9 10	Interesting	1 2 3 4 5 6 7 8 9 10
Caring	1 2 3 4 5 6 7 8 9 10	Silly	1 2 3 4 5 6 7 8 9 10
Thoughtful	1 2 3 4 5 6 7 8 9 10	Creative	1 2 3 4 5 6 7 8 9 10
Smart	1 2 3 4 5 6 7 8 9 10	Helpful	1 2 3 4 5 6 7 8 9 10
Funny	1 2 3 4 5 6 7 8 9 10	Fun	1 2 3 4 5 6 7 8 9 10

YOUR TOTAL POINTS SCORE IS ____ OUT OF 100. THAT MAKES YOU A SUPERMOM!

1. ....

2. ....

3. ....

4. ....

5. ....

MOM IS ALWAYS SO BUSY, BUT SHE ALWAYS HAS TIME FOR...

WE HAVE LOTS OF LAUGHS,

....
....
....
....
....
....
....
....
....

BUT THIS REALLY MADE US LAUGH A LOT!

WHAT MOVIES
DO YOU LIKE?

Mom's favorite movies

1. ....
2. ....
3. ....
4. ....
5. ....

What I think of them

....
....
....
....
....

My favorite movies

1. ....
2. ....
3. ....
4. ....
5. ....

What Mom thinks of them

....
....
....
....
....

stick your photo here

REMEMBER WHEN WE WENT TO

....

....

....

....

....

....

....

....

....

....

THE TOP 5 THINGS
YOU'VE TAUGHT ME

How to make a ....

How to cook ....

How to play ....

How to use ....

How to ....

HOW WELL CAN YOU DO THESE THINGS?

Color the stars from left to right.

Play on a games console ☆☆☆☆☆

Use a G.P.S. ☆☆☆☆☆

Create a playlist of our favorite songs ☆☆☆☆☆

Search the Internet for funny video clips ☆☆☆☆☆

Buy shoes online ☆☆☆☆☆

Use a smartphone to share photos ☆☆☆☆☆

Buy a new item of clothing in less than 20 minutes ☆☆☆☆☆

Beat Dad at .... ☆☆☆☆☆

Do a trick on my bike ☆☆☆☆☆

Make my favorite dessert ☆☆☆☆☆

stick your photo here

PLEASE DON'T EVER
DO THESE THINGS IN PUBLIC!

1. ....
2. ....
3. ....
4. ....
5. ....
6. ....

YOU LOVE TO SING THESE SONGS OUT LOUD

sounds pretty good

sounds OK

sounds nothing like the original

1. .... ☐ ☐ ☐

2. .... ☐ ☐ ☐

3. .... ☐ ☐ ☐

4. .... ☐ ☐ ☐

5. .... ☐ ☐ ☐

stick your photo here

IF IT WEREN'T FOR ME,
YOU WOULD...

	TRUE	FALSE
Have no gray hair	◯	◯
Not know how to play computer games	◯	◯
Get to sleep on the weekend	◯	◯
Watch your favorite TV shows when you want	◯	◯
Spend more time shopping	◯	◯
Smile less	◯	◯
....	◯	◯
....	◯	◯
....	◯	◯
....	◯	◯

DID YOU REALLY HAVE...?

Draw Mom's old hairstyles on these head outlines.

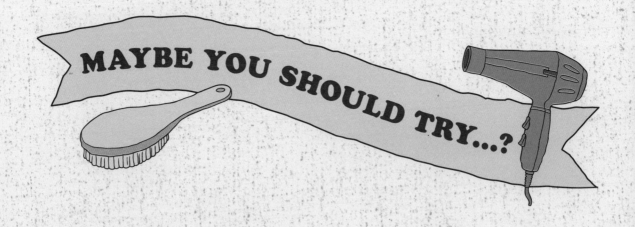

MAYBE YOU SHOULD TRY...?

Draw the hairstyles you'd like Mom to try.

MOM'S PET PEEVES

Cleaning up my mess ☐

Getting lost ☐

Being late ☐

Loud music ☐

Dirty dishes ☐

.... ☐

.... ☐

.... ☐

stick your photo here

WHEN MOM IS...

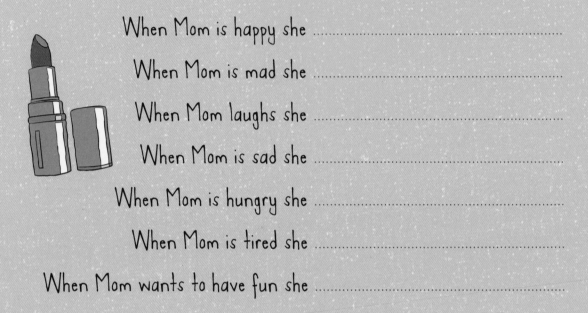

When Mom is happy she ....

When Mom is mad she ....

When Mom laughs she ....

When Mom is sad she ....

When Mom is hungry she ....

When Mom is tired she ....

When Mom wants to have fun she ....

stick your photo here

MOM RARELY GETS TO CHOOSE WHAT'S ON THE TV BUT

SHE HAS TO WATCH

....
....
....

MOM'S TV RATINGS

	really likes	likes	pretends to like	dislikes
SPORTS	☐	☐	☐	☐
CARTOONS	☐	☐	☐	☐
REALITY TV	☐	☐	☐	☐
CLASSIC MOVIES	☐	☐	☐	☐
THE NEWS	☐	☐	☐	☐

SOMETIMES WE DO SILLY THINGS AND DECIDE NOT TO TELL ANYONE.

This was one of those silly things!

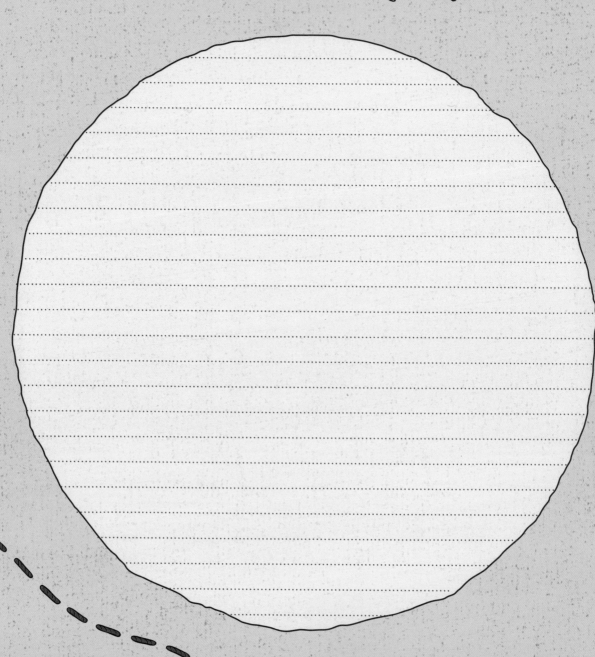

KIND

THOUGHTFUL

CRANKY

HAPPY

FUNNY

A COFFEE CUP OF YOUR CHARACTER!

SERIOUS

PATIENT

COOL

SILLY

WONDERFUL

HELPFUL

Look at these words and think of some of your own. Think of Mom and what she's like and divide the coffee into segments to match how these different characteristics make up her personality.

stick your photo here

I ADMIRE **YOU** BECAUSE...

1. ....

2. ....

3. ....

4. ....

5. ....

MOM'S SPEEDY CHART

Color in the different clock faces to show how long it takes Mom to do each activity.

 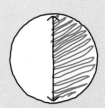  

Super fast
(15 mins)

Fast enough
(30 mins)

Slow
(45 mins)

Forever
(60 mins +)

  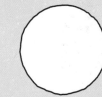

SHOWER

DO HAIR

**PUT ON
MAKEUP**

**CHOOSE
OUTFIT**

 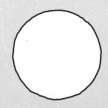 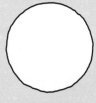 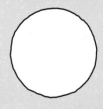

**CHOOSE
SHOES**

**GET
DRESSED**

**PACK
PURSE**

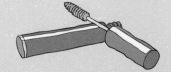 

IN YOUR
PURSE
I KNOW
I WOULD
FIND...

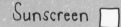

Loose change	☐	Sunscreen	☐
Tissues	☐	Makeup	☐
Diary	☐	Book	☐
Cell phone	☐	Snacks	☐
Keys	☐	Tweezers	☐
Driver's license	☐	Hand cream	☐
Perfume	☐	Nail file	☐
Hand sanitizer	☐		

THE BEST THINGS YOU'VE EVER MADE FOR ME

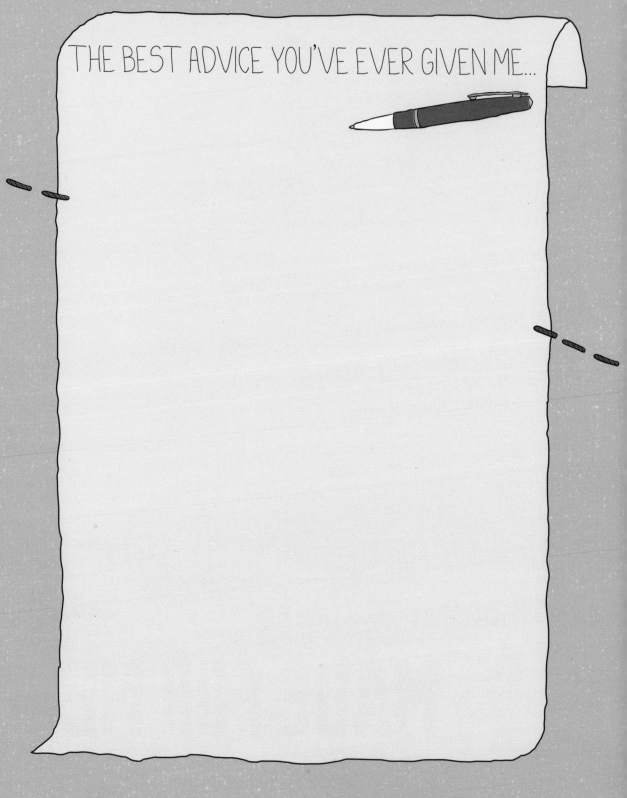

THE BEST ADVICE YOU'VE EVER GIVEN ME...

I LOVED THIS VACATION

FOOD CRITIC RATES MOM'S FOOD!

Gourmet standard

Go back for seconds

Good enough

Just about OK

Rather go hungry

Spaghetti
Steak
Pasta
Apple pie
Scrambled eggs
Chicken salad wrap
Chocolate cake
Fruit salad
Pizza
Pancakes

stick your photo here

THINGS I LOVE DOING WITH YOU

1. ....

2. ....

3. ....

4. ....

5. ....

IF YOU HAD A WHOLE DAY TO YOURSELF, YOU WOULD DO THESE THINGS

MORNING

....
....
....
....
....
....
....
....
....
....

AFTERNOON

....
....
....
....
....

NIGHT

....
....
....
....
....
....
....
....
....
....
....
....
....

I WISH I'D TAKEN A PHOTO WHEN...

Draw what happened at this event.

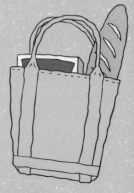

MOM'S LIKES AND DISLIKES

Working ☹ 😐 ☺   Going for lunch ☹ 😐 ☺

Carpooling ☹ 😐 ☺   Reading ☹ 😐 ☺

Dancing ☹ 😐 ☺   Singing ☹ 😐 ☺

Cooking ☹ 😐 ☺   Doing laundry ☹ 😐 ☺

Exercising ☹ 😐 ☺   .... ☹ 😐 ☺

Watching TV ☹ 😐 ☺   .... ☹ 😐 ☺

Shopping ☹ 😐 ☺   .... ☹ 😐 ☺

Cleaning ☹ 😐 ☺   .... ☹ 😐 ☺

....

....

....

....

....

....

....

....

....

....

....

....

....

....

....

YOU DRIVE ME CRAZY WHEN...

What we have in common

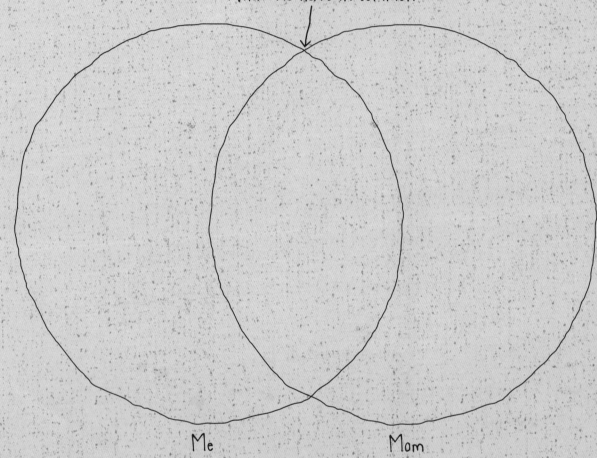

Me

Mom

WE HAVE THESE THINGS IN COMMON

MOM DOING A SILLY POSE FOR THE CAMERA

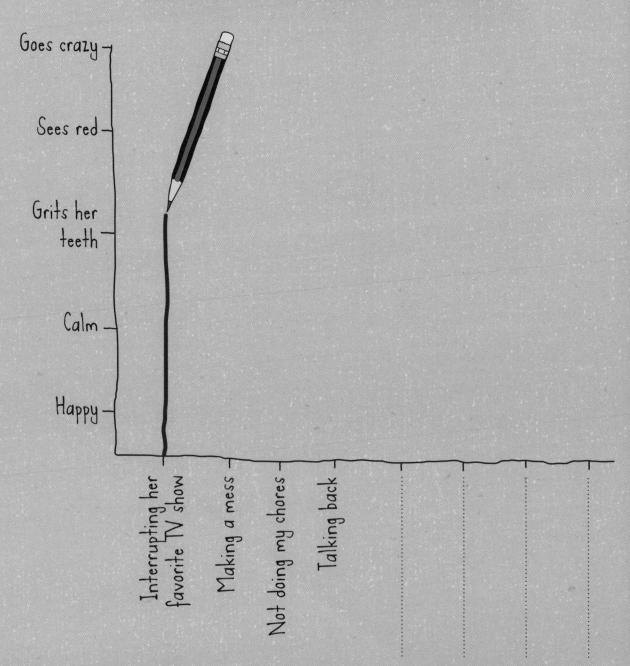

stick your
photo here

YOU REMIND ME OF THESE ACTRESSES

MOM'S FAVORITE
RECIPE

THINGS YOU LIKE TO DO WITH ME ON A RAINY DAY

....

....

....

....

....

....

....

stick your photo here

MY FAVORITE ADVENTURE WITH MOM

1. ....
2. ....
3. ....
4. ....
5. ....

MOM'S GREAT AT...

IF I WERE IN CHARGE OF MOM'S CLOSET, I'D KEEP

....

....

....

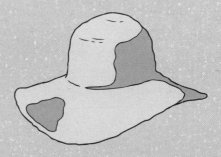

....

....

....

....

BUT I'D DONATE THESE TO A THRIFT STORE

stick your photo here

WE STILL
NEED TO DO
THESE THINGS
TOGETHER

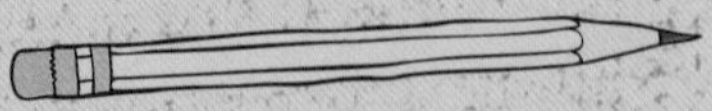

IN MOM'S KITCHEN,
THERE IS ALWAYS

✓

Something cooking ☐

Leftovers in the refrigerator ☐

A newspaper ☐

Cookies ☐

No dishes in the sink ☐

A radio or TV blaring ☐

Today's mail ☐

Coffee in the pot ☐

Cake ☐

Cell phone switched on ☐

Laptop ☐

Car keys ☐

.... ☐

.... ☐

I REMEMBER WHEN

WHY YOU MEAN THE WORLD TO ME...

YOU AND ME NOW

GREAT MOM!

NUMBER 1 MOM

WORLD'S BEST MOM

YOU'RE THE BEST

FANTASTIC MOM!

SUPER MOM

I LOVE YOU MOM

Let's bake

Let's go for a ride

Let's go dancing

Let's go shopping

Let's bake

Let's go for a ride

Let's go dancing

Let's go shopping